I0605745

ICONIC NATIONAL PARKS

ZION NATIONAL PARK

BY ANGELA LIM

Core Library

An Imprint of Abdo Publishing
abdobooks.com

Cover image: Zion National Park is the third-most visited national park in the United States.

abdobooks.com

Published by Abdo Publishing, a division of ABDO, PO Box 398166, Minneapolis, Minnesota 55439.

Printed in the United States of America, North Mankato, Minnesota.
052025
092025

Cover Photo: Nico De Pasquale Photography/Stone/Getty Images
Interior Photos: Ziga Plahutar/E+/Getty Images, 4–5; Shutterstock Images, 6, 13, 28, 31 (map, tool), 31 (light, first aid, tent), 31 (water), 31 (fire), 43 (bottom), 45; Red Line Editorial, 9; iStockphoto, 10–11; Daniel Flesher/iStockphoto, 14; Brandon Leavell/500px/Getty Images, 18–19; Daniel McConnell/National Park Service, 20; B. T. Hamilton/National Park Service, 23; Phil Armitage/Flickr, 25; Nickolay Stanev/Shutterstock Images, 26–27; Ruslan Ivantsov/Shutterstock Images, 31 (hat, jacket); Marko Blagoevic/Shutterstock Images, 31 (food); Russ Bishop/Alamy, 32; Bill Crnkovich/Alamy, 34; National Park Service, 36–37; Steve Cukrov/Shutterstock Images, 42 (top); Ken Koskela/Alamy, 42 (middle); Design Pics/Alamy, 42 (bottom); Sanjay Kaul/Shutterstock Images, 43 (top); Kawin Towe/Shutterstock Images, 43 (middle)

Editor: Christa Kelly
Series Designer: Marley Richmond

Library of Congress Control Number: 2024948996

Publisher's Cataloging-in-Publication Data

Names: Lim, Angela, author.
Title: Zion National Park / by Angela Lim
Description: Minneapolis, Minnesota: Abdo Publishing, 2026 | Series: Iconic national parks | Includes online resources and index.
Identifiers: ISBN 9781098297220 (lib. bdg.) | ISBN 9798384919742 (ebook)
Subjects: LCSH: Zion National Park (Utah)--Juvenile literature. | Bluffs (Landforms)--Juvenile literature. | Natural monuments--Juvenile literature. | Scenic landscapes--Juvenile literature. | National parks and reserves--Juvenile literature.
Classification: DDC 979.2--dc23

CONTENTS

CHAPTER ONE

HIKING ANGELS LANDING

Eric wiped sweat from his forehead as he took a big swig from his water bottle. He and his family were hiking to Angels Landing in Zion National Park. The trail was steep and rugged. Eric took some time to catch his breath and look out at his surroundings.

Eric was blown away by how beautiful the landscape was. Sandstone canyons lay all around him. They were striped with bands of brown, pink, and gold.

Park rangers issue permits for nearly 200,000 people to hike Angels Landing each year.

Angels Landing reaches an elevation of nearly 5,800 feet (1,800 m).

Once they finished taking in the scenery, Eric and his family continued hiking. They were nearing the end of the trail. He held onto the chain railing and followed his older brother. Eric's mom was behind him. His dad was waiting below at Scout Lookout. He was afraid of heights. Eric thought it was good that he had stayed behind. The trail kept getting steeper and narrower.

After a difficult climb, Eric reached the summit with his mom and brother. They looked around in shock. It felt as if they were on top of the world. A carpet of green plants grew along the Virgin River, which now seemed small and far away. Colorful rock walls and towers surrounded them in all directions. Eric thought he could look at the view forever and never grow tired of it. He knew he would remember his time at Zion National Park for the rest of his life.

DARK SKIES

Zion National Park is an International Dark Sky Park. This means the park strives to limit light pollution. Light pollution occurs when artificial light sources scatter light into the atmosphere. This causes the night sky to look brighter and hazier, making it difficult to see stars. Using fewer lights and adding shields to lights so they shine downward can limit light pollution. This allows park visitors to see stunning views of the Milky Way. It also protects nocturnal animals that rely on the cover of darkness.

VISITING ZION

Zion National Park protects approximately

232 square miles (601 sq km) of land in southwestern Utah. It is one of the most popular national parks in the United States. More than 4.5 million visitors come each year. The park is famous for its breathtaking scenery and colorful canyons.

The Virgin River runs through the park, creating an ever-shifting landscape. Near the river, ferns cling to the steep faces of canyon walls. At higher elevations, juniper and evergreen trees grow.

Zion National Park also preserves pieces of ancient American Indian cultures.

PERSPECTIVES

WHEN TO VISIT

The most popular time to visit Zion is from April to September. This is when trails are the most accessible. However, visitors will have to deal with crowds and high temperatures. The park is less crowded in the fall and winter, but trails may be dangerous to hike due to snow and ice. Jorge Hernandez works at Zion. He says the park is worth visiting at any time of year. "There's no bad time to visit Zion. Depending on the season, you'll see Zion completely different."

ZION NATIONAL PARK

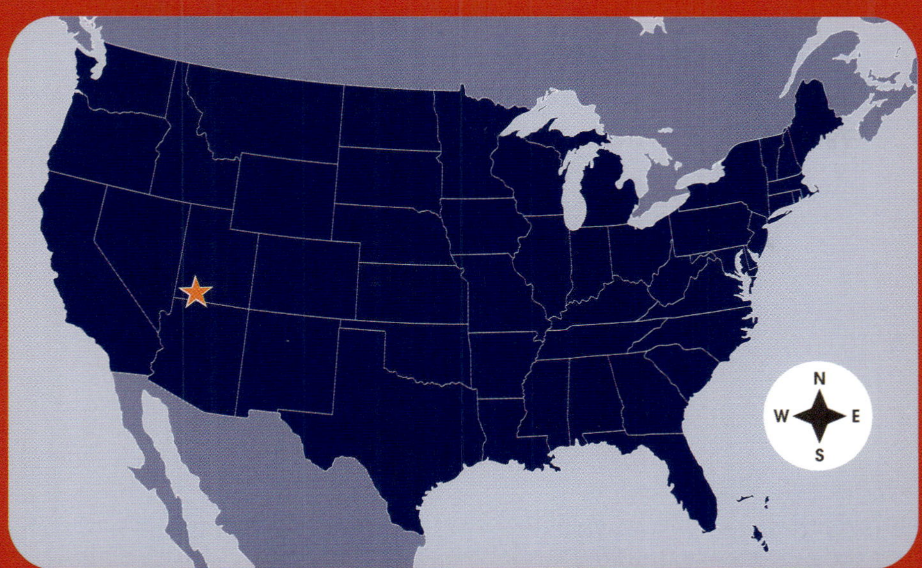

Zion National Park is located in southwestern Utah. It is one of Utah's five national parks. Why might some states have so many national parks while others have none? How could a state's geography impact the number of parks it has?

People have lived in the area for thousands of years. Visitors can see artifacts and ancient rock art called petroglyphs from early civilizations.

Some people visit Zion to spot wildlife. Others visit to explore the outdoors. Adventure seekers enjoy the thrill of rock climbing and canyoneering. With its stunning landscapes and rich history, Zion National Park offers visitors a variety of exciting activities.

CHAPTER TWO

HISTORY OF ZION NATIONAL PARK

Zion National Park sits on the edge of the Colorado Plateau. This land formation is home to towering cliffs striped with red bands. The colors come from the presence of iron in the stone.

The rock layers of Zion National Park started forming about 270 million years ago. At this time, Zion was a relatively flat basin around sea level. The basin was surrounded by mountains. Streams running down from the mountains deposited sediment into the basin.

Zion is known for its colorful rock formations.

The sediment included many types of sand, gravel, and mud. These heavy sediments layered on top of each other, causing the Zion basin to sink.

Over time, the geology of the area began to change. Mineral-rich waters trickled through the layers of sediment. The pressure of the layers and the presence of the new minerals caused the sediment to become rock such as limestone, shale, and sandstone.

The rock layers rose from sea level in a process called uplift. Erosion helped shape the landscape as the rock layers were pushed upward. Water sources, such as the Virgin River, carved deep canyons into the rock. Strong winds chipped away at the cliff faces. Erosion continues to change Zion National Park today.

HUMAN HISTORY

The first people arrived in the Zion area about 12,000 years ago. They were hunters and gatherers. The Ancestral Pueblo were the descendants of these

The Virgin River has been cutting through the Zion region for 13 million years.

early people. They grew maize, beans, and squash. Archaeologists have found artwork such as baskets and pottery made by the Ancestral Pueblo.

The Ancestral Pueblo left the area in the 1200s. This was likely because of an ongoing drought that made agriculture challenging. Today, visitors to Zion can see cliff houses and petroglyphs that the Ancestral Pueblo left behind.

Visitors to Zion can hike to Petroglyph Canyon to see ancient rock art.

Other American Indian nations moved into the region, including the Ute, Paiute, Shoshone, Goshute, and Navajo. Zion National Park remains an important place for these American Indian nations today. For example, the Paiute Indian Tribe of Utah has a spiritual and cultural connection to the land. The nation plays a role in preserving nature within the park.

The first European Americans to settle in the region were members of a religion called The Church of Jesus Christ of Latter-day Saints. They were led to the land by Brigham Young in the late 1800s. They named the region Zion, after the Hebrew word for "sanctuary" or "refuge."

ESTABLISHING THE PARK

John Wesley Powell worked for the US government as a land surveyor. In 1872, he surveyed the area that would become Zion National Park. Powell listed the canyon's name as Mukuntuweap. This is a Paiute word that means "straight canyon."

Land surveyors urged the US government to protect the area. In 1909, President William Howard Taft agreed. He established Mukuntuweap National

SACRED DEFENSE

National parks sit on land that once belonged to American Indian nations. The development of national parks drove many American Indians from their homelands. The Sacred Defense National Parks and Monuments Initiative provides a way for national park visitors to support the nations connected with the parks. Money donated under the initiative goes to the American Indian nations native to the region. Zion National Park was one of the first 14 national parks to be included in the initiative.

Monument to preserve the canyons and the region's natural environment. The monument included 16,000 acres (6,500 ha) of land.

President Woodrow Wilson expanded the size of the monument in 1918 and renamed it Zion National Monument. A year later, it was designated a national park. In 1956, the Kolob Canyons area was added to the park.

Today, the National Park Service maintains Zion National Park. It provides educational resources for visitors to learn about the park's history. It also works to protect the plants and animals that live within the park.

PERSPECTIVES

TAFT'S PROCLAMATION

Zion National Park was first protected by President William Howard Taft. Taft was impressed by the park's beauty. He made an official proclamation in 1909 to preserve the "labyrinth of remarkable canyons with highly ornate and beautifully colored walls, in which are plainly recorded the geological events of past ages."

STRAIGHT TO THE SOURCE

David Treuer is an Ojibwe writer and professor at the University of Southern California. He wrote an opinion piece for the *Atlantic* in 2021 explaining why he believes national park lands should be returned to American Indian nations. Treuer said:

> *The national parks are sometimes called "America's best idea," and there is much to recommend them. They are indeed awesome places, worthy of reverence and preservation, as Native Americans like me would be the first to tell you. But all of them were founded on land that was once ours, and many were created only after we were removed, forcibly, sometimes by an invading army and other times following a treaty we'd signed under duress.*

Source: David Treuer. "Return the National Parks to the Tribes." *Atlantic*, 12 Apr. 2021, theatlantic.com. Accessed 3 July 2024.

WHAT'S THE BIG IDEA?

Take a close look at this passage. What is the main connection being made between national parks and American Indian nations? How does this information influence the way you view national parks?

CHAPTER THREE

PLANTS AND ANIMALS

Zion National Park has desert, river, and woodland ecosystems. The landscape varies depending on elevation. Each ecosystem is home to different types of plants and animals.

More than 1,000 plant species can be found in Zion National Park. Some plants grow in challenging areas, such as in rocky crevices along steep cliff faces. Water from the Virgin River splatters onto low cliff walls, providing moisture to ferns, mosses, lilies, and

Despite Zion's arid climate, trees, flowers, and mosses thrive in the region.

Many of Zion's wildflowers, such as shooting stars, grow by rivers and springs.

other plants. The greenery provides shelter and food for many animals, including insects and amphibians.

Wildflowers are another group of plants that provide beauty and support Zion's ecosystems. Many of the wildflowers in the park bloom in the early spring when rainfall is the most plentiful. They grow mainly in meadows at the bottom of the valley.

Succulents grow in the driest parts of the park. These plants have thick, fleshy stems and leaves. Cacti are a subgroup of succulents that have spines. Several species of cacti grow in the park.

YUCCA

Five types of yucca grow in Zion National Park. Yuccas are succulents with waxy leaves, which limit water loss from evaporation. They have deep roots that allow them to get water from far underground. Yucca plants bloom in spring and early summer. Their white flowers are pollinated only by the yucca moth. The yucca moth also depends on yucca plants for survival. The moths lay their eggs on yucca plants. The moth larvae eat the seeds of yucca fruit once they hatch.

THE ANIMALS OF ZION

Zion National Park is home to many types of animals. The tarantula hawk is a wasp that is found in the park. The wasp drinks nectar from milkweed plants.

Female tarantula hawks can sting and paralyze tarantulas, earning the species its name. The female drags a paralyzed tarantula to its burrow and lays its eggs inside the tarantula. The wasp larvae eat the tarantula when they hatch.

The Virgin River is home to six native species of fish, three of which are endemic. This means they're not found anywhere else. The flannelmouth sucker is the largest fish endemic to the Virgin River. It is between 12 and 25 inches (30 and 64 cm) when full-grown. The fish has fleshy lips that help it feed on algae.

Amphibians also rely on Zion's waterways. They breed and lay eggs in the water. Amphibians hibernate during the cold winter months and become active when temperatures are warmer. Seven types of amphibians can be found in Zion National Park, including the tiger salamander. It is the only salamander in the park.

Zion National Park is home to 16 species of lizards and 13 types of snakes. During the winter months, reptiles in the park burrow underground. They enter a hibernation-like state called brumation.

The Great Basin rattlesnake is the only venomous snake in Zion. It has a triangular head and a light brown

The Great Basin rattlesnake eats birds, reptiles, amphibians, and small mammals.

body with dark splotches. This snake is adapted to the desert environment and can go months at a time without water. It gets almost all the water it needs from the prey it eats.

Nearly 300 species of birds can be found in Zion National Park. Some of these species are migratory. Others stay in the park year-round. Some birds, such

PERSPECTIVES

RESPECTING WILDLIFE

Many people go to Zion National Park to see the region's wildlife. However, visitors must be careful to respect the animals they see. Animals can carry diseases. They may also become aggressive if they feel threatened. Nicole Frey works with wildlife management at Zion National Park. She talked about the importance of respecting wildlife. She said one major way to respect wildlife is to not feed animals. Feeding animals puts them in danger. It can make them more aggressive and more likely to seek out human contact.

as the Steller's jay and the black-capped chickadee, are commonly spotted throughout the year. Zion is also a sanctuary for endangered birds such as the California condor. This bird nearly went extinct in the 1980s, with only about 20 of them left in the world. Today, the bird's numbers are up to about 400.

Visitors to Zion National Park also have the chance to see some of the 68 mammal species found in the park. Rock squirrels and mule deer are among the most common.

California condors can often be seen soaring above Angels Landing.

Wildlife watchers should also be aware that some mammals are more active at night. Bobcats, porcupines, and bats are all nocturnal.

FURTHER EVIDENCE

Chapter Three describes the animals that live in Zion National Park, including the California condor. What was one of the main points of this chapter? What evidence is included to support this point? Read the article at the website below. Does the information on the website support the main point of the chapter? Does it present new evidence?

CALIFORNIA CONDORS

abdocorelibrary.com/zion-national-park

CHAPTER FOUR

RECREATION

Hiking is a popular activity at Zion National Park. It is important to prepare for hikes by wearing proper gear and bringing necessary equipment such as food, water, and waterproof clothing. Even short hikes can be strenuous in extreme temperatures.

The Narrows is a popular trail at the park. It follows the Virgin River as it winds through canyons. In some places, the canyons are only 20 feet (6 m) wide. The cliffs on either side

Zion National Park has more than 90 miles (140 km) of trails.

Visitors hiking the Narrows should wear closed-toed shoes and clothes that dry quickly.

are about 1,000 feet (300 m) tall. The trail begins as a paved, wheelchair-accessible path, but after about one mile (1.6 km), hikers must wade through the Virgin River. The hike is 9.4 miles (15.1 km) round trip. A longer, 16-mile (26 km) hike is available with a permit.

Water levels in the Narrows vary depending on the amount of rainfall and snowmelt. Hikers should prepare to wade through water that is about knee-high to thigh deep. Occasionally, water may be up to chest level.

Visitors hoping to hike the Narrows should pay close attention to the weather. Thunderstorms may create flash floods. Flash floods can cause the height of the Virgin River to rise in seconds. This can be deadly. People should avoid the Narrows if a storm is coming.

PERSPECTIVES

PREPARING FOR HIKES

Hiking can be dangerous without the proper supplies. Andrew Herrington is a survival expert. He said that the biggest mistake people make is being ill-prepared for hikes. Hikers at Zion should wear shoes with ankle support and traction. Visitors should also bring food and water on hikes. Protection from the sun is important too.

The Angels Landing trail is another noteworthy hike at Zion National Park. Angels Landing offers panoramic views of Zion Canyon. The rock overhang was named by a Christian minister who thought the spot was so high that only angels would be able to land there.

Hiking Angels Landing is incredibly strenuous. The trail stretches 5.4 miles (8.7 km) with a 1,488-feet (454 m) change in elevation. It takes about four to five hours to complete. Near the summit, the trail is only a few feet wide with steep drop-offs on both sides.

Many people come to Zion to hike Angels Landing. To ensure safety and prevent overcrowding, Zion National Park requires hikers to obtain a permit to complete the hike. People can enter a seasonal lottery to get a permit. They can also enter a day-before lottery system if they would like to hike the trail the following day.

Zion National Park also has many easy and moderate hikes, such as the Middle Emerald Pools Trail. This trail is 2.2 miles (3.5 km) round trip. It winds through pinyon–juniper woodlands and offers views of waterfalls cascading into shallow pools. Some hikers spot wildlife along the trail. The pools are important sources of water for the park's animals, so hikers are not allowed to swim in the water.

THE TEN ESSENTIALS

The National Park Service recommends that all visitors pack the ten essential items when exploring a national park. Why are these items important? What other items might you need when hiking at Zion?

1. Navigation

2. Sun protection

3. Insulation

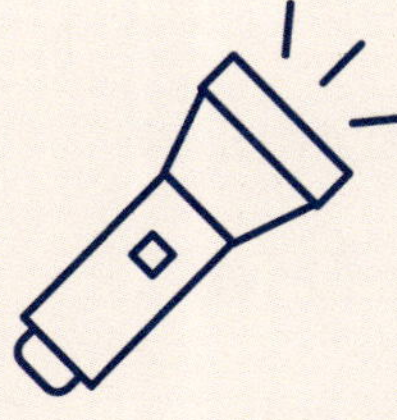

4. Illumination

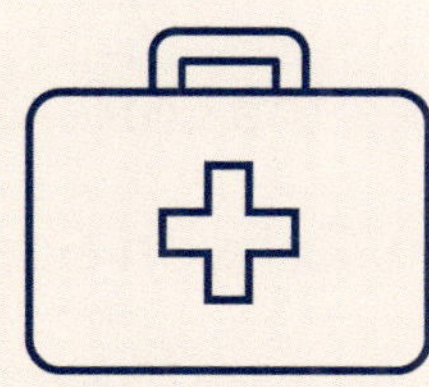

5. First-aid supplies

6. Fire

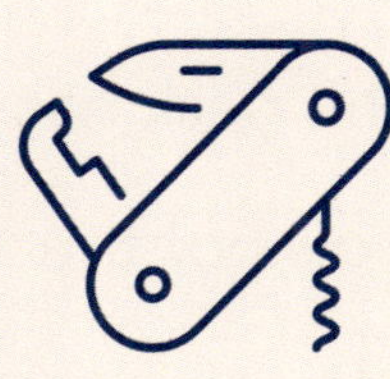

7. Tools

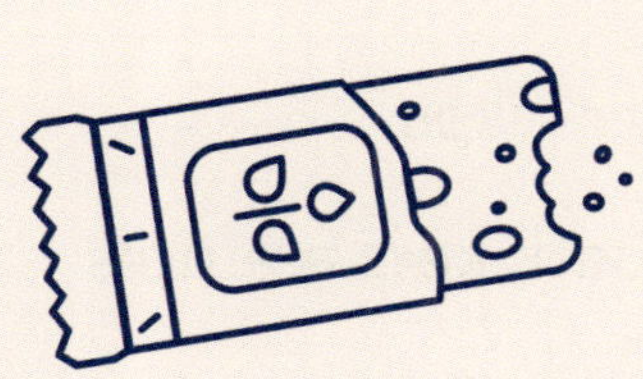

8. Food

9. Water

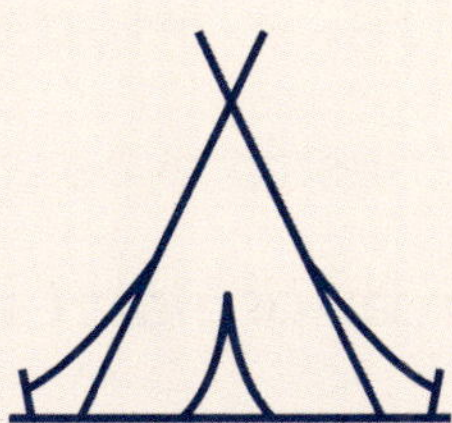

10. Emergency shelter

Most of the climbing routes in Zion should be attempted only by experienced climbers.

EXPLORING BY VEHICLE

Some people explore Zion National Park from their cars. The park has several scenic drives that offer beautiful views of the landscape. The Zion Canyon Scenic Drive allows visitors to see stunning views of Zion Canyon. During peak tourist season, park shuttles are the only vehicles allowed on the road. Visitors can ride the shuttles to access some of Zion's popular hikes.

The Kolob Canyons section of the park also features a scenic drive. The route is about five miles (8 km).

It offers views of colorful canyons and access to trails in the area.

CLIMBING AND CANYONEERING

Climbing and canyoneering are other ways of exploring Zion National Park. The best times for climbing are in the spring and autumn. During the summer months, high temperatures can make these activities incredibly strenuous. Rain is also more likely in the summer. Water dampens rocks and makes them more likely to break off.

Canyoneering and overnight climbs require wilderness permits. Climbers and canyoneers need to

ROCK FALLS

Climbers and hikers in Zion National Park must look out for rock falls. Heavy rains can cause rocks to move, triggering a rockslide. Water may seep into crevices in the rock and freeze when temperatures drop. This causes rocks to expand and break apart. One rock fall can lead to more rock falls in the area, so it is important to listen to park staff about whether it is safe to enter an area. Sections of the park may be closed due to active rock falls.

The trail to Lava Point Overlook takes only two minutes to hike.

pay attention to closures that may affect their plans. They should also stay on well-established routes to avoid disturbing wildlife and damaging plants.

DAWN, DUSK, AND NIGHT

Sunrise and sunset highlight the beauty of Zion National Park. Many people enjoy the park's views at these times.

Lava Point Overlook is a great location to watch the sun rise and set over the park's canyons and plateaus. Canyon Overlook is another ideal location to watch the sunrise. During sunset, Pa'rus Trail is a popular hike. Visitors can see the Watchman, a mountain in the park, basking in the fading light.

At night, people can camp at one of the three campgrounds in the park. Reservations are needed to camp within the park, and spots fill up quickly. It is recommended to make a camping reservation at least six months in advance.

EXPLORE ONLINE

Chapter Four talks about ways to stay safe while exploring Zion National Park. The article at the website below goes into more depth on this topic. Does the article answer any of the questions you had about how to stay safe at Zion?

SAFETY

abdocorelibrary.com/zion-national-park

CHAPTER FIVE

CARING FOR THE PARK

Park staff helps protect the landscapes and wildlife within Zion National Park. One way park workers do this is by replanting native plants. Zion has a native plant nursery that houses thousands of plants from dozens of native species. Plants from the nursey can be replanted in the wild. Park workers transfer these plants to areas that have been damaged by wildfires, erosion, or human traffic. The park also waters heavily trafficked areas to help plants grow.

Park workers collect seeds from Zion's native plants. Rangers grow the seeds and use the plants to restore the park's ecosystems.

WILDERNESS PERMITS

In 2010, 2.6 million people visited Zion National Park. The number of annual visitors rose to more than five million in 2021. In order to protect the landscape, the staff at Zion National Park started issuing permits for certain activities. These permits help limit overcrowding. Wilderness permits are required for activities such as canyoneering and camping. In 2022, Zion began requiring a permit for hiking Angels Landing. Permits are also required for the full 16-mile (26 km) hike through the Narrows.

Park visitors share a responsibility to protect Zion. People should stay on designated trails. This prevents damage to fragile areas. Hikers should also clean their shoes to prevent seeds from other places from being carried into the park. Bringing new seeds into the park can spread invasive species that may outcompete native plants.

CLIMATE FRIENDLY

Zion has been designated as a Climate Friendly Park. As a Climate Friendly Park, workers monitor the park's greenhouse gas emissions and strive to improve sustainability. Zion National Park also educates visitors about climate change and how individuals can help reduce their impact on the environment.

One way that Zion National Park works toward sustainability is by providing recycling receptacles and educating visitors about recycling. Recycling helps reduce the amount of waste in landfills. A 2016 study found that 53 percent of the waste in trash cans at Zion could have been recycled.

In 2023, Zion National Park began using electric shuttles to transport park visitors. It was the first national park in the country to fully transition to electric vehicles. These zero-emissions vehicles reduce greenhouse gas emissions and help limit traffic within the park.

WHAT VISITORS CAN DO

Visitors play an important role in protecting Zion. They can keep the park healthy by leaving it as it was when they entered. This means properly disposing of waste, staying on trails, and respecting wildlife. Visitors should also never take artifacts or natural objects as souvenirs. These treasures should be left for others to enjoy.

PERSPECTIVES

MAINTAINING ZION

In 2023, the road leading to Kolob Canyons collapsed due to erosion. Construction workers began rebuilding the road with the aim to make it more stable than it was before. They laid a netlike blanket called a geotechnical grid over the soil to help slow erosion. Jonathan Shafer is a public affairs specialist at Zion. He said, "Our goal when we're done here is that we keep the park a park, we protect this place, and we also maintain access so that folks are able to come here and enjoy it."

Zion National Park has diverse ecosystems, beautiful views, and a rich history that must be protected for future generations. With so much to see and do, Zion National Park is a treasured American icon. Together, visitors and park rangers can preserve the region for future generations.

STRAIGHT TO THE SOURCE

Zion National Park is one of the most-visited national parks in the United States. However, the park is understaffed for the number of visitors it sees each year. Jeff Bradybaugh was the park superintendent in 2023. He spoke about the challenges of taking care of the park:

> *We are glad that many people are getting outside to enjoy their parks and public lands, but it does present challenges for park staff protecting park resources, maintaining public health, and sustaining facilities. We continue to protect Zion so that the millions of visitors who travel to experience the park's iconic scenery . . . continue to enjoy their time here.*

Source: Julie Jag. "At Zion National Park, Too Many People, Too Little Management." *Salt Lake Tribune*, 3 May 2023, sltrib.com. Accessed 24 Oct. 2024.

BACK IT UP

The author of this passage is using evidence to support a point. Write a paragraph describing the point the author is making. Then write two or three pieces of evidence the author uses to make the point.

PARK LANDMARKS

Angels Landing is a steep rock formation. Visitors can hike to the top for panoramic views of Zion Canyon.

The **Emerald Pools** are named for their emerald waters. Hiking trails take visitors to each of the three pools.

The **Narrows** is a gorge at the base of Zion Canyon. It's a popular hiking trail that takes visitors through the Virgin River.

The **Temple of Sinawava** marks the beginning of the hike to the Narrows. It is a large clearing at one end of Zion Canyon with hanging gardens and waterfalls.

The **Court of the Patriarchs** is a cluster of three mountains. They can be viewed from an overlook on Zion Canyon Scenic Drive.

Kolob Canyons are higher in elevation than Zion Canyon. This section of the park offers views of steep canyons and free-standing arches.

STOP AND THINK

Surprise Me

Chapter Three discusses the plants and animals of Zion National Park. After reading this book, what two or three facts about Zion's ecosystems and wildlife did you find most surprising? Write a few sentences about each fact. Why did you find each fact surprising?

Say What?

Studying national parks can mean learning a lot of new vocabulary. Find five words in this book you've never heard before. Use a dictionary to find out what they mean. Then write the meanings in your own words and use each word in a new sentence.

You Are There

This book describes a variety of activities to do in Zion National Park. Imagine you are in Zion National Park. What activity do you try? Write a letter home describing your experience. Be sure to add plenty of details to your letter.

Another View

This book talks about the American Indians who are native to the Zion National Park area. As you know, every source is different. Ask a librarian or another adult to help you find another source about one of these nations. Write a short essay comparing and contrasting the new source's point of view with that of this book's author. What is the point of view of each author? How are they similar and why? How are they different and why?

GLOSSARY

canyoneering
a sport that involves exploring canyons by climbing and rafting

ecosystem
a community of organisms living together and interacting

emission
a gas released into the air

erosion
the gradual wearing away of land by external forces, such as wind or water

geology
the study of the earth and rocks

land surveyor
a person who records an area's boundaries and geological features

plateau
a large area of land with a flat surface that is higher than the surrounding land

sediment
solid material that settles in a new place

uplift
an increase in elevation of an area of land due to natural shifts of tectonic plates, the large pieces of land that make up the top layer of earth's surface

ONLINE RESOURCES

To learn more about Zion National Park, visit our free resource websites below.

Visit **abdocorelibrary.com** or scan this QR code for free Common Core resources for teachers and students, including vetted activities, multimedia, and booklinks, for deeper subject comprehension.

Visit **abdobooklinks.com** or scan this QR code for free additional online weblinks for further learning. These links are routinely monitored and updated to provide the most current information available.

LEARN MORE

Lassieur, Allison. *The National Parks Encyclopedia*. Abdo, 2023.

London, Martha. *Utah*. Abdo, 2023.

Ward, Alexa. *America's National Parks*. Lonely Planet, 2024.

INDEX

About the Author

Angela Lim is an MFA student in poetry at Indiana University.